INSPIRE COMPUTING

International

Workbook   YEAR **3**

Sabiha Munshi

Series editor: Paul Clowrey

Pearson

Published by Pearson Education Limited, 80 Strand, London, WC2R 0RL.
www.pearson.com/international-schools

Copies of official specifications for all Pearson Edexcel qualifications may be found on the website:
https://qualifications.pearson.com

Text © Pearson Education Limited 2023
Project managed and edited by Just Content
Designed and typeset by PDQ
Picture research by Integra
Original illustrations © Pearson Education Limited 2023
Cover design © Pearson Education Limited 2023
Cover illustration © Beehive/Andrew Pagram

The right of Sabiha Munshi to be identified as the author of this work has been asserted by her in accordance with the Copyright, Designs and Patents Act 1988.

First published 2023

25 24 23
10 9 8 7 6 5 4 3 2 1

British Library Cataloguing in Publication Data
A catalogue record for this book is available from the British Library

ISBN 978 1 292 40432 5

Printed in Slovakia by Neografia

The author and publisher would like to thank the following individuals and organisations for permission to reproduce photographs, illustrations, and text:
KEY (t - top, c - center, b - bottom, l - left, r - right)

123RF: Neyro2008 25, Agnieszka Murphy 76t; Pearson Education Ltd: PDQ Digital Media Solutions Ltd 16, 23, 32b, 49; Scratch: Scratch is a project of the Scratch Foundation in collaboration with the Lifelong Kindergarten group at the MIT Media Lab. It is available for free at https://scratch.mit.edu, Creative Commons Attribution-ShareAlike license 65, 66t, 66c, 67, 68, 66b, 69t, 69c, 69b, 70t, 70b, 71, 72, 75, 76tc, 76c, 76b, 77t, 77c, 77b, 78, 80, 89t, 89bt, 89bc, 89bb, 90t, 90b, 94, 95, 96tl, 96cl, 96c, 96cr, 97, 98, 99, 103t, 103tl, 103tr, 103bl, 103br; Shutterstock: Jane Kelly 7, BNP Design Studio 12, Naum 24, Macrovector 50, Labib Retroman 113, WilleeCole Photography 114t, Labib Retroman 121.

All other images © Pearson Education

Contents

Welcome to Inspire Computing

We are all living in a continually evolving digital world. By supporting learners in becoming confident and knowledgeable users of technology we can ensure you are prepared for the future.

Inspire Computing makes important topics accessible for all learners. You will understand how to stay safe online while still enjoying the freedom to explore the World Wide Web. You will delve deeper into understanding algorithms through creative approaches, exploring networks and systems, and create and film exciting animation projects!

Each topic includes easy to understand theory, real-world examples, and ideas for further investigation. You will also have the chance to show off your knowledge and understanding through supportive assessments and student checkpoints!

Unit 4

Algorithms and programming (part 1)

In this unit, you will learn more about algorithms and programming. You will learn about sequences and how important they are to programming. You will begin the unit by exploring content in Scratch online, before playing a maze game and using directional language to direct a sprite to a target. You will find bugs in your sequences and debug your code as you progress through the lessons. You will plan, design and make your own maze to test your skills. Finally, you will use advanced programming blocks to program your sprite.

62

Lesson 1
Reviewing algorithms

I. When talking about an algorithm, which of the following describes the sequence?

A   the first command ☐

B   the order of instructions ☐

C   the last command ☐

D   the number of commands ☐

2. **a)** What is a convention?

_____

b) Using a sensible convention, rewrite the following algorithm in a shorter way:

```
forward 10
turn left
forward 30
turn right
```

63

Unit 6   End-of-unit assessment

Unit 6
End-of-unit assessment

I   You are working on a presentation in school and must save your work in the class area. What should you include in your file name?

A   your pet's name ☐

B   the day of the week ☐

C   your best friend's name ☐

D   your name ☐

(I mark)

2   A folder inside another folder is called a…

A   subfolder ☐

B   internal folder ☐

C   infolder ☐

D   super folder ☐

(I mark)

3   A student is organising some files on their computer. To the right are the new subfolders.

📁 Music
📁 Photos
📁 School work
📁 Scratch Programs
📁 Videos

a)   The student has done some research that they will use in a class presentation. Which folder should they save the file in?

_____

120

Unit 6   End-of-unit assessment

Unit 6 Checkpoints

I can save work regularly and keep information secure.	🙂 ☐ 😐 ☐ 🙁 ☐	
I can use sensible file names.	🙂 ☐ 😐 ☐ 🙁 ☐	
I can organise files into directories, folders and subfolders.	🙂 ☐ 😐 ☐ 🙁 ☐	
I understand how to use usernames and passwords to secure data.	🙂 ☐ 😐 ☐ 🙁 ☐	
I can choose and use different software applications.	🙂 ☐ 😐 ☐ 🙁 ☐	

122

vii

Unit 1
The World Wide Web

In this unit, you will learn about the World Wide Web (WWW) and how search engines work. You will learn tips about searching on the internet, as well as how to research and take notes. Then you will use these skills in your own project. You will be researching facts for a non-chronological report about a current learning topic. You will store the information you find in a document in note form, using word processing software. You will be able to use these notes to make a presentation project to show your class.

Lesson 1
What is the World Wide Web?

1. WWW means:

   A   What? Where? When?

   B   World Wide Web

   C   Which World Works

   D   Watch World Wide

2. Which of the following statements is **incorrect**?

   A   The World Wide Web describes all the documents stored online.

   B   A group of connected web pages is called a website.

   C   The internet is the same as the World Wide Web.

   D   The internet describes all the connected devices around the world.

3. What piece of software do we normally use to access the internet?

   A   a search engine

   B   a word processor

   C   a web window

   D   a web browser

4. Describe three ways a search engine uses keywords to search the internet.

I _____

_____

2 _____

_____

3 _____

_____

5. What word is used to describe the order of results presented by a search engine?

_____

Lesson 2
Using a search engine

I. Why should you not always trust the results at the top of a search engine that are marked 'Ad'?

_____

_____

_____

2. Describe two things you should do and two things you should **not** do if you come across something that makes you feel sad or worried:

Should do	Should not do

3.   Can you name three popular search engines?

1 _____

2 _____

3 _____

4.   Is the following statement true or false? Tick the correct box.

You cannot copy and paste website content when using a tablet.

☐   True   ☐   False

Lesson 3
Taking notes

1. What does the word 'plagiarism' describe?

A using someone else's work and pretending it is your own ☐

B writing something that is untrue ☐

C avoiding advertisements when searching the web ☐

D writing something in your own words ☐

2. You have been asked to paraphrase a story on a news website. What does 'paraphrase' mean?

_____

_____

_____

3. Describe two tips for anyone taking notes.

    1 _____

    _____

    2 _____

    _____

4. Make notes from the text below into four brief bullet points:

    The internet is the network of connected devices that allows us to communicate with each other across the world. The World Wide Web is all the documents, called web pages, that are stored on the internet. We call a group of connected web pages a website. Many people confuse the internet with the World Wide Web.

    ■ _____

    ■ _____

    ■ _____

    ■ _____

Lesson 4
Formatting text

1. Match the formatting terms to the correct descriptions.

bold	This makes words slant to the right.
underline	This is small shapes or icons before words.
italic	This makes words stand out by making them darker.
bullet points	This puts numbers before the words in a list.
numbered list	This makes words stand out by putting a line underneath the letters.

2. List three types of text alignment.

1 _____

2 _____

3 _____

3. Is the following statement true or false? Tick the correct box.

The shape and size of bullet points cannot be changed.

☐ True   ☐ False

4. Open your Student Book and find an example of where the following has been used. Write down the page number.

a bold text _____

b bullet points _____

c text alignment _____

d numbered list _____

Lesson 5
Researching offline

1. **a)** Describe the difference between online and offline research.

_____

_____

_____

b) Give two examples of each:

Online	Offline

2. Describe the difference between fiction and non-fiction text.

_____

_____

_____

3. Match the non-fiction parts of a book to the correct descriptions.

contents	This gives definitions of the key words in the book.
glossary	This is at the start of the book and tells the reader what is in the book.
index	This lists all the important words in the book and says what page they are on.

4. Find a non-fiction book and look at the index in the back. Choose two words that interest you. Use the index to help you find them in the book. Write some short notes about each word. Share them with a partner or group.

I _____

_____

_____

2 _____

_____

_____

Lessons 6 and 7
Non-chronological reports

1. **a)** Describe the difference between chronological and non-chronological events.

_____

_____

_____

_____

b) Give an example of a text for each type.

Chronological	Non-chronological

2. List four features you could use when writing a report:

1 _____

_____

2 _____

_____

3 _____

_____

4 _____

_____

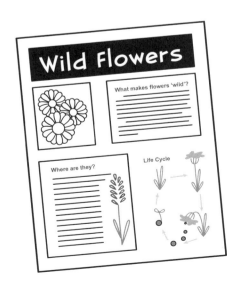

3. Is the following statement true or false? Tick the correct box.

It is a good idea to use a question as a heading in a report.

☐ True   ☐ False

4. **a)** Which of these is the odd one out?

A a dictionary ☐

B a children's encyclopaedia ☐

C a book about wildflowers ☐

D a storybook ☐

b) Explain your answer.

_____

_____

5. Look at the pictures below and circle the set of books that are non-chronological.

Lessons 8 and 9
Presentation skills

1. As well as text, describe three elements that could be used to create a presentation.

1 _____

2 _____

3 _____

2. Instead of pages, a presentation contains…

A panels ☐

B windows ☐

C slides ☐

D posters ☐

3.   Match the presentation terms to the correct descriptions.

animation

This controls how one slide moves to the next.

hyperlink

This controls how objects appear, move and disappear.

transition

This is used to jump to any point in a presentation or to a web page.

4.   What is the name used to describe the people you are making a presentation for?

A   specific crowd ☐

B   target audience ☐

C   focus group ☐

D   people of interest ☐

Lesson 10
Practising and performing your presentation

1. Describe three things to include when giving constructive feedback.

   1 _____

   2 _____

   3 _____

2. Describe two tips for giving a good presentation.

   1 _____

   _____

   2 _____

   _____

I enjoyed your speech because you spoke clearly.

3. Draw a picture of someone giving a good or bad presentation. Label the things that you think make it good or bad.

4. Write in the speech bubbles two good things you could say when you are giving constructive feedback.

Unit 1
End-of-unit assessment

I   What is the full name for the WWW?

    A   Wired Web World   ☐

    B   World Wide Web   ☐

    C   Wireless World Wonder   ☐

    D   Working Web Wide   ☐

(I mark)

2   Some people make sure their website appears at the top of search engine lists by...

    A   using paid-for search engine adverts   ☐

    B   adding lots of graphics   ☐

    C   filling their website with adverts   ☐

    D   removing all photos   ☐

(I mark)

3 Copying someone else's work and pretending it is your own is known as...

    A paraphrasing ☐

    B pestering ☐

    C plagiarism ☐

    D pilfering ☐

(I mark)

4 Moving a subheading to the right of a page is done using which formatting tool?

    A bold ☐

    B numbering ☐

    C italic ☐

    D alignment ☐

(I mark)

5 Which of these is a way to format the way text looks on the screen?

    A copy ☐

    B crop ☐

    C border ☐

    D font ☐

(I mark)

Unit 1 Checkpoints

I know what the WWW and the internet are.	😊 ☐ 😐 ☐ ☹ ☐
I can use a search engine well.	😊 ☐ 😐 ☐ ☹ ☐
I know how to research on the internet and make notes.	😊 ☐ 😐 ☐ ☹ ☐
I know what online and offline research is.	😊 ☐ 😐 ☐ ☹ ☐
I know how to make a word processing document and presentation.	😊 ☐ 😐 ☐ ☹ ☐

Unit 2

Podcasts

In this unit, you will learn all about podcasts. You will start by learning what a podcast is, what types are the most popular and how they are made. You will learn about audio editing and make a range of different podcasts for your listeners: an interview, a book review, a foreign language lesson and a news report. You will need to plan your episodes before making them. Feedback will be given to help you make improvements to your podcasts as you get more practice using the software.

Lesson 1
What is a podcast?

I. What is a podcast?

_____

_____

_____

_____

2. Listen to three different podcasts, and write their names below.

I _____

2 _____

3 _____

3. Write three tips for anyone thinking about making a podcast.

1 _____

_____

2 _____

_____

3 _____

_____

4. Which of the following would you not normally listen to a podcast on?

    A   smartphone   ☐

    B   digital radio   ☐

    C   smart TV   ☐

    D   tablet   ☐

Lesson 2
Recording a podcast jingle

1. **a)** What is a podcast jingle?

_____

_____

b) Describe three things a jingle might contain.

1 _____

_____

2 _____

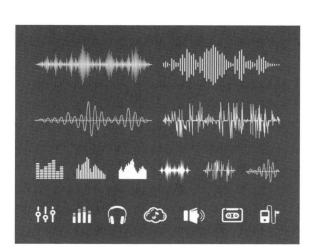

_____

_____

_____

3 _____

_____

_____

_____

2. Multiple audio recordings in the same file are called...

A   beats   ☐

B   tracks   ☐

C   echoes   ☐

D   objects   ☐

3. Draw the commonly used icon shapes for the following functions when recording audio.

a) Stop

b) Play

c) Record

4. When creating a podcast jingle, you should only use music that...

A   is loud

B   you have permission to use

C   is quiet

D   is recorded by a famous musician

Lesson 3
Planning an interview

1. If the person asking the questions is the interviewer, what word describes the person being interviewed?

_____

2. **a)** What is the difference between an open and a closed question?

_____

_____

_____

b) Describe an example of each for an interview about smartphones.

An open question: _____

_____

A closed question: _____

_____

What do you like best about your smartphone?

Well...

3. Match the questioning terms to the correct descriptions.

follow-up question	This sets the scene and helps the interviewee feel comfortable.
starter question	This is useful if the interviewee only gives short answers.
question plan	This is used to build on a previous answer.
spare questions	This is the order of questions from start to finish.

4. Are the following questions open or closed? Tick the correct boxes.

a   Do you like cats?   ☐ Open   ☐ Closed

b   What is your favourite hobby?   ☐ Open   ☐ Closed

c   Tell me about your holiday.   ☐ Open   ☐ Closed

d   How old are you?   ☐ Open   ☐ Closed

e   What do you like about school?   ☐ Open   ☐ Closed

Lesson 4
Recording an interview

I.   Imagine you are going to interview someone famous. Write three questions to ask them.

I will interview _____.

I will ask them...

1

2

3

2. Write three tips for recording a good interview.

1 _____

_____

2 _____

_____

3 _____

_____

3. Match the audio-editing terms to the correct descriptions

delete		This removes a selected part so it can be pasted into another point in the track.
cut		This turns one part of a track into two at a selected point.
trim		This removes a selected part of the track.
split		This shortens the track at either the start or the end.

4. Is the following statement true or false? Tick the correct box.

☐ True   ☐ False

Tracks in the same file can be moved independently without changing other tracks.

Lessons 5 and 6
Recording a book review

I. What should be kept level, to prevent a podcast getting louder or quieter?

_____

2. If the volume is not loud enough, describe two things that you could do.

I _____

_____

2 _____

_____

3. Think about your favourite books. List your Top 3 and briefly say why you like them.

1 _____

_____

_____

_____

2 _____

_____

_____

3 _____

_____

_____

4. You have been asked to record a book review podcast. List four things you might include.

1 _____

2 _____

3 _____

4 _____

5. What is it important **not** to do when describing the book?

A   give the name of the author ☐

B   name any of the characters ☐

C   describe any bad parts ☐

D   tell the whole story ☐

I. What word is used to describe changing the pitch of your voice (making it higher or lower)?

     A   feedback   ☐

     B   volume   ☐

     C   expression   ☐

     D   intonation   ☐

2. What word is used to describe feelings being shown in a voice?

     A   intonation   ☐

     B   volume   ☐

     C   expression   ☐

     D   pitch   ☐

3. Describe three tips for recording a foreign language podcast.

1 _____

_____

2 _____

_____

3 _____

_____

4. a) Which foreign language are you using for your podcast from Lessons 7 and 8 in the Student Book?

_____

b) Write a list of some foreign language words you want to use in your podcast.

Tip

Make sure they are fun and interesting for someone else to learn!

_____   _____

_____   _____

_____   _____

_____   _____

Hello!

Hola!

Ni Hao!

Ciao!

Shalom!

Lesson 9
Planning a news report

1. Which of the following would you describe as formal language?

☐ Good afternoon. Thank you for downloading our daily news podcast.

☐ Hiya! It's news time! Here's what's happening today in the world!

2. Write three tips for someone planning a formal world news podcast.

1 _____

_____

_____

_____

2 _____

_____

_____

_____

3 _____

_____

_____

_____

3. A friend said, "Stick to the facts, not what you think about them."
Why did they say this about recording a news report?

_____

_____

_____

4. List two things that are often used at the end of a news report.

1 _____

2 _____

And finally...

To end this news report...

5. Which of the words below would not be used in a formal news report?

A "Hey!" ☐

B "Hello." ☐

C "Welcome..." ☐

D "My name is..." ☐

Lesson 10
Recording a news report podcast

1. Describe three examples of a warm-up activity for your voice before recording a podcast.

1 _____

_____

2 _____

_____

3 _____

_____

2. In the table of words below, circle the eight most important words when it comes to planning and recording a podcast.

plan	slowly	rush	loud music
mumble	test	audience	plagiarise
multiple voices	argue	clarity	expression
intonation	edit	confuse	bad jokes

3. Listen to a partner's news report from Lesson 10 of the Student Book, and ask them to listen to yours.

a) Give your partner constructive feedback about their news report. Remember to be kind and respectful!

I liked _____

_____.

You were good at _____

_____.

Next time, maybe you could _____

_____.

It would be better if _____

_____.

My favourite thing about your news report was _____

_____

_____.

b) When you have listened to your partner's constructive feedback about **your** news report, write what you would change next time.

I enjoyed your news report because...

_____

_____

_____

_____

_____

Unit 2
End-of-unit assessment

I   A student is writing a script for their podcast. Which is the best application for them to use?

   A   a presentation application

   B   an internet browser application

   C   a word processing application

   D   an email application

(I mark)

2   A student is going to collect some sound clips of playground noise to use in their podcast. Which type of device could they use for this task?

   A   tablet or smartphone

   B   speakers

   C   desktop computer

   D   radio

(I mark)

3 Which of the following is **not** an example of a closed question?

    A   What is your favourite day of the week? ☐

    B   What year were you born? ☐

    C   What do you like about school? ☐

    D   How many hours are there in a day? ☐

                                                      (1 mark)

4 What is the name of the podcasting software that you used in the Student Book?

_____

                                                      (1 mark)

5 What does the round icon normally mean in an audio-editing app?

    A   plays a track ☐

    B   edits a track ☐

    C   rewinds a track ☐

    D   records a track ☐

                                                       (1 mark)

Unit 2 Checkpoints

I know what a podcast is.	☺ ☐ 😐 ☐ ☹ ☐
I can choose the correct software for podcasting.	☺ ☐ 😐 ☐ ☹ ☐
I know how to use the different features in podcasting software.	☺ ☐ 😐 ☐ ☹ ☐
I know how to plan and make different kinds of podcasts.	☺ ☐ 😐 ☐ ☹ ☐
I can give feedback on other students' work.	☺ ☐ 😐 ☐ ☹ ☐

Unit 3

Keeping myself safe

In this unit, you will learn how to be safe, responsible and show respect online. You will think about your own online habits before learning about appropriate contact, content and conduct. You will learn how to think about all three elements so that you can stay safe when you are online. To show your learning, you will make your own e-safety comics. This comic will show others how they can be kind online, as well as how to recognise and report unacceptable behaviour from other people.

I. What do we mean when we use the word 'e-safety'?

_____

_____

_____

_____

2. List three examples of personal information.

I _____

2 _____

3 _____

3. Imagine you are going to post a photo of yourself online. List three things that you shouldn't show. Remember, they can be in the background and very small, so think carefully!

I _____

2 _____

3 _____

4. Is the following statement true or false? Tick the correct box.

> Your digital footprint is all the data you leave behind when using the internet, from comments to your search history.

☐ True   ☐ False

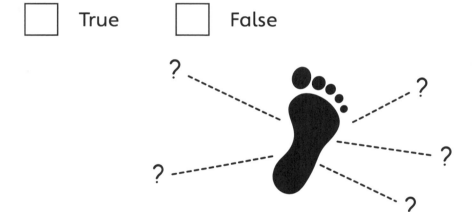

5. Are the following examples online or offline activities? Tick the correct boxes.

Example	Online	Offline
Watching a downloaded TV show on a tablet		
Video calling your grandparents		
Streaming a podcast		
Using the calculator application on your smartphone to help with homework		

Lesson 2
Creating a document about online safety

1. List four applications that you have used, and for each one give an example of why you have used it.

Application	Example of use

2. a) Name three applications that you could use to make an online safety document.

1 _____

2 _____

3 _____

b) Which application will you use for your own document?

I will use _____.

3. Once you have decided which application to use, draw a mind map about your online safety document. Think about what the document will look like. Will it have pictures? Headings? Will you use colours? What is the title?

My online safety
document

4. Write two tips for creating interesting digital content.

    1 _____

    _____

    2 _____

    _____

Lesson 3
How well can we know someone online?

I. Is the following statement true or false? Tick the correct box.

> It is impossible to hide your identity when communicating online.

☐ True   ☐ False

Who's that?

2. Give two pieces of advice for a friend communicating with someone online who they don't know in person.

I _____

_____

2 _____

_____

3. Is the following statement true or false? Tick the correct box.

It is possible to use an online photo that does not look like you.

☐ True   ☐ False

4. Match the online safety terms to the correct descriptions.

alter ego	The name you use to log onto any online system or account.
online identity	An alternate personality someone uses that is different from their real one.
username	How people represent themselves on the internet

5. Talk to a partner or group. Is everything you see online real? Is it always easy to tell the difference between something real or made up?

Is everything you see online real?

Lesson 4
Introduction to comics

1. Name two comic books that you have heard of, seen or read.

1 _____

2 _____

2 Match the comic book features to the correct descriptions.

panel	Shows the thoughts of the character.
thought bubble	Describes moving or sound effects that cannot be easily drawn.
action word	A box containing a drawing of part of the story.
caption	Shows the words said by a character.
speech bubble	A description of the scene or background information about the story.

3. Write two popular topics for comic books.

1 _____

2 _____

4. Choose a subject or story that interests you and draw a short comic strip about it in the space below. Use your imagination and make it fun!

Lesson 5
Being safe and responsible online

1. **a)** Describe two good things about communicating online.

1 _____

_____

2 _____

_____

b) Describe two problems with communicating online.

1 _____

_____

2 _____

_____

2. **a)** What is an emoji?

_____

_____

b) Draw three examples of popular emojis.

3. Give two examples of each of the following when communicating online.

Staying safe	Being responsible	Being respectful

4. Imagine you see something that worries you online. It might be a scary picture or a nasty message, for example. What should you do?

A   click on it / answer it ☐

B   show it to all your friends ☐

C   show it to an adult you trust ☐

D   ignore it ☐

Lesson 6
Making a comic about being kind

1. List three things you need to decide when planning a comic.

1 _____

2 _____

3 _____

2. Describe one good thing and one bad thing for each device when using them to create a comic.

Device	Good	Bad
Tablet		
Smartphone		
Desktop computer		

3. Write some words that remind you about being kind online. You could use them in your comic strip from Lesson 6 of the Student Book.

4. Draw some pictures that remind you about being kind online. Could you use some of them in your comic strip?

Lessons 7 and 8
Recognising and reporting unacceptable behaviour

1. Complete the three sentences below. Use the words in the word bank to help you.

Word bank
conduct   contact   content

a) The _____ you make with other people should be appropriate.

b) Be responsible with the _____ you make and share online.

c) Show respect in the way you _____ yourself.

2. In the scenarios below, tick whether it is an example of inappropriate contact, content or conduct.

Device	Contact	Content	Conduct
A stranger on your games console chat asks if you can speak to them on another message app.			
A friend on a group messaging app starts asking others for rude names to describe their teachers.			
You are sent a link to a video with a much higher age rating than your own.			

3. Is the following statement true or false? Tick the correct box.

It is easy to go back and erase any online messages that you regret sending.

☐ True   ☐ False

4. You receive a message from someone you have never met or spoken to before. What should you do?

A   don't reply and show it to a trusted adult   ☐

B   reply and then tell a trusted adult   ☐

C   reply and continue a conversation with them   ☐

D   don't reply and tell your friends   ☐

Hi, we like the same sport. Meet me in the park so we can play.

A ☺

Lessons 9 and 10
Giving and responding to feedback on your comics

1. Write three types of feedback.

   1 _____

   2 _____

   3 _____

2. What should constructive feedback include?

   _____

   _____

   _____

I liked …

Next time you could…

3. Is the following statement true or false? Tick the correct box.

   You should always explain all types of feedback, not just the negative ones.

   ☐ True   ☐ False

4.   **a)** What is annotation?

_____

b) Why is it useful when improving your work?

_____

_____

5.   Draw a mind map about the feedback you received for your comic strip. Include the positive and the negative, then add some ideas for how you might improve it.

My comic strip feedback

Unit 3
End-of-unit assessment

I   What does 'e-safety' mean?

   A   playing games in real life   ☐

   B   keeping myself safe online   ☐

   C   playing games online   ☐

   D   buying something online   ☐

                                                        (I mark)

2   A good friend has shared an embarrassing photo of you to
    other students. What should you do?

   A   share a photo that they will not like with your friends   ☐

   B   block your friend   ☐

   C   talk to your friend and explain how you are feeling   ☐

   D   nothing, it is their photo to share   ☐

                                                        (I mark)

3 If someone makes a hurtful comment to you online, what should you do first?

    A ask for an apology ☐

    B tell a trusted adult ☐

    C ask why they have said it ☐

    D say something hurtful back ☐

                                          (1 mark)

4 Write one example of content you can find online.

_____

                                          (1 mark)

5 Which of these are online activities? Tick two choices.

    A going to a shop and buying a book ☐

    B watching a video that you recorded at the park ☐

    C checking your school website ☐

    D going to the beach ☐

    E video streaming famous mountains from all over the world ☐

                                          (2 marks)

Unit 3 Checkpoints

I can make safe, responsible and respectful choices when using technology.	☺ ☐ 😐 ☐ ☹ ☐
I can recognise unacceptable behaviour online and offline.	☺ ☐ 😐 ☐ ☹ ☐
I know that I should report any worries about content, contact and conduct, both online and offline.	☺ ☐ 😐 ☐ ☹ ☐
I can create comics for different purposes using applications.	☺ ☐ 😐 ☐ ☹ ☐
I can give and receive feedback.	☺ ☐ 😐 ☐ ☹ ☐

Unit 4

Algorithms and programming (part 1)

In this unit, you will learn more about algorithms and programming. You will learn about sequences and how important they are to programming. You will begin the unit by exploring content in Scratch online, before playing a maze game and using directional language to direct a sprite to a target. You will find bugs in your sequences and debug your code as you progress through the lessons. You will plan, design and make your own maze to test your skills. Finally, you will use advanced programming blocks to program your sprite.

Lesson 1
Reviewing algorithms

1. When talking about an algorithm, which of the following describes the sequence?

   A   the first command ☐

   B   the order of instructions ☐

   C   the last command ☐

   D   the number of commands ☐

2. **a)** What is a convention?

   _____

   b) Using a sensible convention, rewrite the following algorithm in a shorter way:

   ```
   forward 10
   turn left
   forward 30
   turn right
   ```

3.   Write some shorthand conventions, along with their meanings, below.

Shorthand   Meaning

_____   _____

_____   _____

_____   _____

_____   _____

_____   _____

_____   _____

_____   _____

_____   _____

_____   _____

_____   _____

4.   Is the following statement true or false?
     Tick the correct box.

| There are no rules for notation and conventions, as long as all the people using them know about them and agree. |

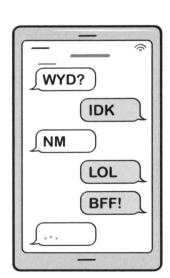

☐ True   ☐ False

Lesson 2
Scratch introduction

1. In the table below, add two similarities and two differences between ScratchJr and Scratch.

What is similar?	What is different?

2. If you open and play an online Scratch game, which command allows you to see how it was built?

A explore

B tutorials

C ideas

D see inside

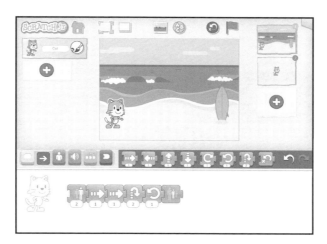

3.   Is the following statement true or false? Tick the correct box.

In Scratch, blocks can be linked together.

☐ True   ☐ False

4.   Label the Scratch features below.

a)

_____

b)

Blue Sky

_____

c)

_____

Lesson 3
Using algorithms

I. Write an algorithm to get from the start to the end of the maze below, collecting only the egg and avoiding the beanbag and the gem.

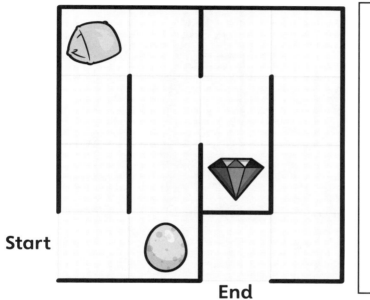

Start

End

2. An error in a program that stops it working is often called a...

    A   spider   ☐

    B   snake   ☐

    C   bug   ☐

    D   pest   ☐

3.   What is the term used to describe finding and getting rid of a program error?

_____

4.   Write an algorithm to get from the start to the end of the maze below and pick up a gem without getting burned. Beware, collecting one gem is more difficult than the other!

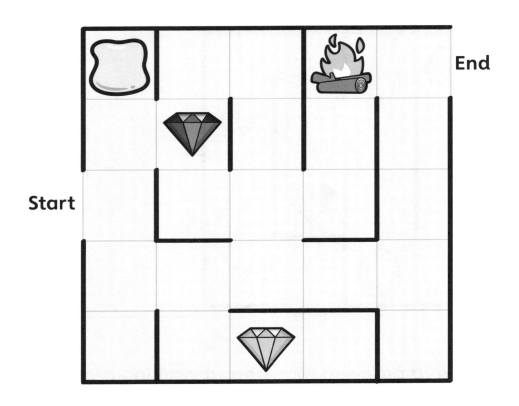

Lesson 4
Programming a sprite

1. Describe the purpose of the following Scratch blocks.

a)

when ⚑ clicked

_____
_____
_____
_____

b)

move 100 steps

_____
_____
_____
_____

c)

turn ↻ 90 degrees

_____
_____
_____
_____

2. Draw the Scratch block that is used to turn left 90 degrees.

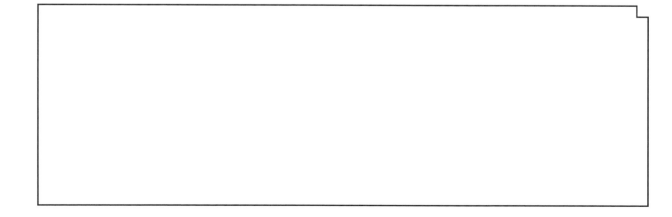

3. When creating an algorithm in Scratch, like the maze example below, what problem might happen when moving the sprite one or two steps?

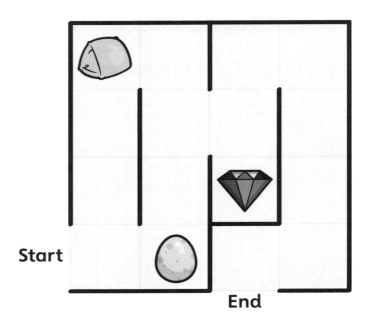

Start

End

_____

_____

_____

4. A 90-degree turn is also known as a...

A   triangle ☐

B   wrong angle ☐

C   right angle ☐

D   left angle ☐

Lesson 5
Using keyboard input

I. Match the Scratch blocks to the correct descriptions.

Events	These are used to make the sprite say messages or to change the background.
Motion	These are used to play built-in or recorded sounds.
Looks	These are used to start programs.
Sounds	These are used to move and rotate the sprite.

2. List three of the ways that sound can be added to a Scratch program.

I _____

_____

2 _____

_____

3 _____

_____

3. What input device do you need to be able to record your own sound?

_____

4. Is the following statement true or false? Tick the correct box.

> Numbers cannot be used as keyboard input commands in Scratch.

☐ True　　　☐ False

5. **a)** Which of the following is a block section in Scratch?

    A Finds ☐

    B Noises ☐

    C Movement ☐

    D Events ☐

b) What does it do?

_____

Lessons 6 and 7
Planning your maze game

1. List three possible ways to design a maze without using a computer.

1 _____

2 _____

3 _____

2. After creating a simple maze design, you have been asked to make it more difficult. Describe two ways you could do this.

1 _____

2 _____

3. **a)** Using the grid provided, design a maze that needs to be solved to get from point A to point B.

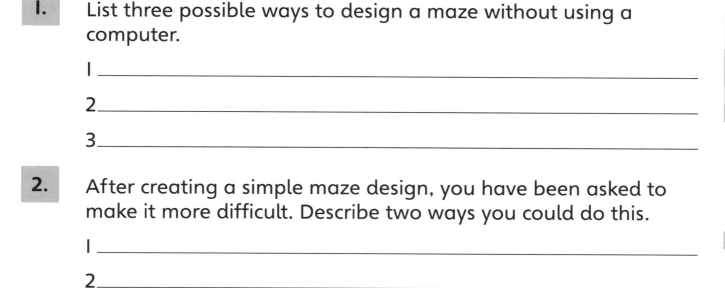

b) Using the convention provided below, write an algorithm solution to the maze.

forward one step = fd 1

turn right = rt

turn left = lt

4. Look again at your maze from question 3. Can you make it more difficult? Redraw it in the grid with some added challenges.

B

A

Tip

If you are stuck, draw a solution path on the grid first, then create a maze around it!

Lesson 8
Making your maze game

I. In Scratch, the background used in a program is called a...

    A   backstage   ☐

    B   backdrop   ☐

    C   back-area   ☐

    D   back-mount   ☐

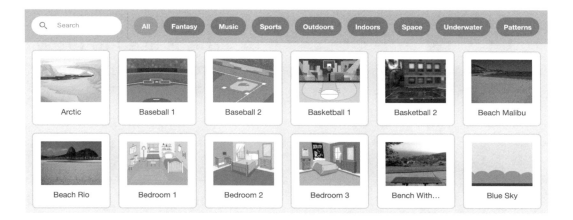

2. Each movement step in Scratch is one pixel. What is a pixel?

_____

_____

3. In Scratch, what is the name of the area that displays your finished program?

_____

4. Here is a simple image made out of pixels. Design your own pixel picture in the grid.

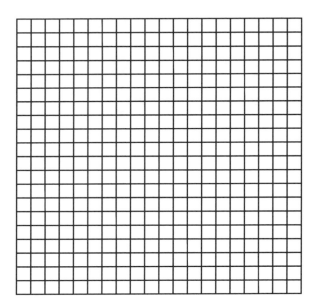

5. Match the Scratch tools to the correct descriptions.

This is used to draw a straight line.

This is used to take a step back if a painting mistake is made.

This is used to choose the line colour.

Lesson 9
Improving your maze game

I. Now you have made your Scratch maze game in Lessons 8 and 9 of the Student Book, describe three possible improvements you could make.

1 _____

_____

2 _____

_____

3 _____

_____

2. Describe what happens to the sprite if the following blocks are used:

a)

_____

b)

_____

c)

_____

3.   Is the following statement true or false? Tick the correct box.

Each Scratch project can only have one backdrop.

☐ True   ☐ False

4.   When moving a sprite using the keyboard or blocks, using a negative value will make it...

A   move sideways   ☐

B   turn left   ☐

C   go backwards   ☐

D   stop   ☐

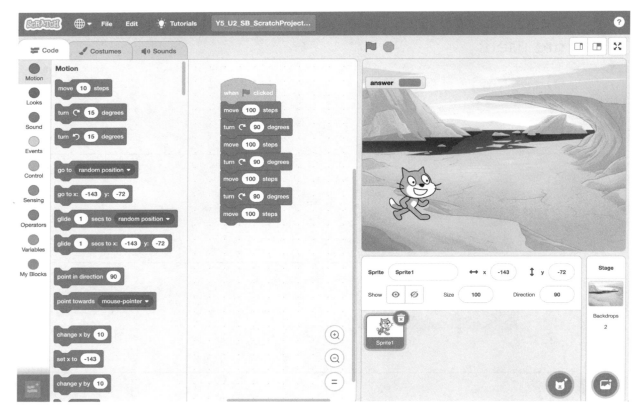

Lesson 10
Playtesting your maze game

1. Describe the meaning of the word 'playtesting'.

_____

_____

_____

2. Which of the following is an example of constructive feedback?

A

This game is too hard!

B

It was too quick to finish.

C

I loved everything about the game!

D

Maybe the game would be longer with more levels?

3. A friend has asked you to playtest their Scratch game. You have to move a spaceship from one side to the other without hitting an asteroid or a black hole.

List three things you could comment on if you were giving constructive feedback on this type of game.

1 _____

2 _____

3 _____

4. There is a bug in the control program shown.

a) What is the bug in the program?

_____

_____

_____

b) How could it be solved?

_____

_____

_____

Unit 4
End-of-unit assessment

I   Writing the command 'turn left 90 degrees' as 'lt' is an example of...

   A   sequencing ☐

   B   shorthand ☐

   C   programming ☐

   D   debugging ☐

(I mark)

2   What is the 'See inside' button for when using Scratch?

   A   to share a photo with your friends ☐

   B   to block your friend ☐

   C   to add another sprite ☐

   D   to look at the sequence of blocks that built the program ☐

(I mark)

3   Find and fixing errors in a program is known as...

   A   debugging

   B   derezzing

   C   deploying

   D   destroying

(1 mark)

4   'When flag clicked' or 'when spacebar pressed' can be found in which Scratch section?

   A   Motion

   B   Events

   C   Looks

   D   Sound

(1 mark)

5   When using the 'move' block in scratch, one step is equal to...

   A   one pixel

   B   one centimetre

   C   one sprite

   D   one backdrop

(1 mark)

Unit 4 Checkpoints

I can find and fix errors in a program.	☺ ☐ / 😐 ☐ / ☹ ☐
I can use notation `fd`, `lt 90` and `rt 90` when writing algorithms.	☺ ☐ / 😐 ☐ / ☹ ☐
I can write algorithms to solve a problem.	☺ ☐ / 😐 ☐ / ☹ ☐
I can use sequencing in programs.	☺ ☐ / 😐 ☐ / ☹ ☐
I can create a maze on Scratch software.	☺ ☐ / 😐 ☐ / ☹ ☐

Unit 5

Algorithms and programming (part 2)

In this unit, you will learn more about programming, direction and movement. You will discover how to make two-dimensional (2D) shapes using algorithms and how to program these using Scratch. You will explore this process by following algorithms that create a shape and debug algorithms to check that they create a shape correctly. You will use the pen tool in Scratch and design your own program and experiment with creating custom blocks. Then, you will use these blocks to create colourful repeating patterns.

Lesson 1
Creating 2D shape algorithms

1. Algorithms are a set of precise...

    A   sequences   ☐

    B   coordinates   ☐

    C   rules   ☐

    D   instructions   ☐

2. You are about to write an algorithm on how to draw a coloured rectangle on a grid. List at least three pieces of essential information you would need to provide.

1 _____

_____

2 _____

_____

3 _____

_____

3. Write clear, precise instructions to create the two rectangles shown below.

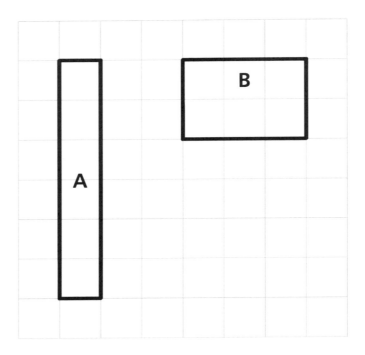

A _____

_____

_____

B _____

_____

_____

4. Add a third shape to the grid in question 3, using the following instructions.

Starting at the bottom right, draw the outline of a black square that is two blocks high and two blocks wide, and colour it in any colour.

Lessons 2 and 3
Drawing 2D shapes

1. Complete the missing two lines from the algorithm below to create a rectangle.

> forward 50
>
> right 90
>
> forward 20
>
> _____
>
> forward 50
>
> right 90
>
> _____

2. Create a similar algorithm to create a square with four sides of 75 steps each.

3. Complete the table below showing the sizes and turn angles of the shapes.

Shape	Number of sides	Turn angle (degrees)
Rectangle		
Triangle		

4. List three tips for predicting what shape an algorithm will produce.

1 _____

_____

2_____

_____

3_____

_____

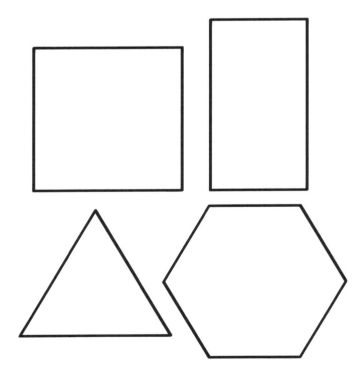

Lesson 4
Creating custom blocks in Scratch

I. What are extensions for in Scratch?

_____

_____

Pen

Draw with your sprites.

2. Match the Scratch tools to their functions.

To start drawing a line on the screen.

To stop drawing a line on the screen.

To add a Scratch extension.

3. Put the steps for creating a custom block into the correct order by numbering them from 1 to 8.

☐ Click on the 'Make a block' button.

☐ Drag the name of your new block from the 'My blocks' section.

☐ Look for the 'Define (block name)' block on the screen.

☐ Carefully save your work.

☐ Go to the 'My blocks' section.

☐ Give your block a suitable name.

☐ Your custom block can be added to any programs.

☐ Attach any blocks you wish to use.

● My Blocks

✏ Pen

My Blocks

Make a Block

Pen

4. Is the following statement true or false? Tick the correct box.

Custom blocks can only be used once in each project.

☐ True   ☐ False

Make a Block

Draw a square

Lesson 5
Finding the correct sequence of instructions

1. The Scratch program below for drawing a rectangle 100 steps wide and 50 steps high is in the wrong order.

   a) Put the blocks into the correct order by numbering them from 1 to 11.

   ☐   `move 100 steps`

   ☐   `turn right 90 degrees`

   ☐   `move 50 steps`

   ☐   `move 100 steps`

   ☐   `pen up`

   ☐   `turn right 90 degrees`

   ☐   `when flag clicked`

   ☐   `move 50 steps`

   ☐   `turn right 90 degrees`

   ☐   `turn right 90 degrees`

   ☐   `pen down`

   b) The rectangle could be created with three 'turn right' blocks, but this program has four. Why has an extra one been added?

   _____

   _____

2. Imagine making a cup of tea when the instruction for stirring or drinking came before adding the hot water! Write three examples in your own life where getting the right commands in the wrong sequence will create the wrong result.

1 _____

2 _____

3 _____

3. Here is a sequence for washing your hands, but it has a bug in it. Can you spot it? What is the correct order?

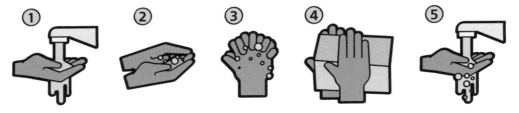

The correct sequence is _____.

4. Here are all the commands you need to put some jam on a slice of bread, but they are in the wrong order. Put the commands into an order that works by numbering them from 1 to 6.

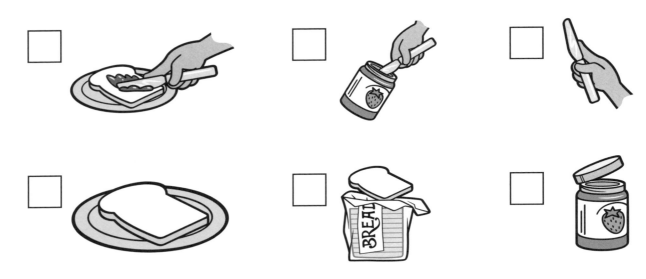

Lesson 6
Breaking down a problem

1. Breaking down a problem into smaller parts in programming is called...

A   sequencing ☐

B   decomposition ☐

C   expression ☐

D   repetition ☐

2. Rather than describing the whole pattern shown below, break it down into shapes and write a set of instructions to create each part at a time. The first one has been done for you.

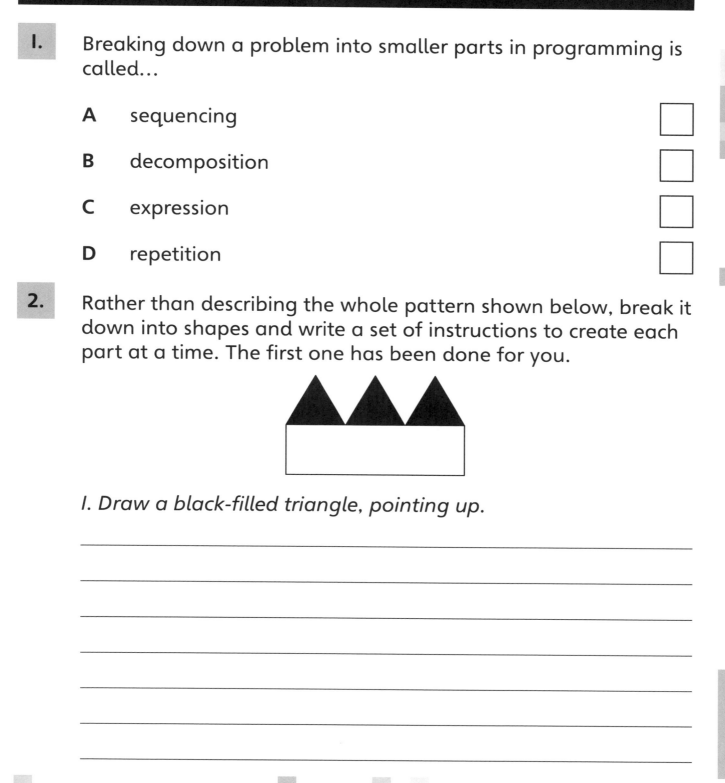

1. Draw a black-filled triangle, pointing up.

_____

_____

_____

_____

_____

_____

3. A classmate is creating an image using multiple shapes in Scratch. Select three pieces of good advice from the list below.

    A   Reduce the size of the sprite. ☐

    B   Avoid using custom blocks to create shapes. ☐

    C   It is better to program graphics with multiple shapes in just one go. ☐

    D   Try and point the sprite in the same direction after drawing each shape. ☐

    E   Use the pen up block to stop drawing and move between shapes. ☐

5. **Is the following statement true or false? Tick the correct box.**

    The centre of the stage in Scratch has the position $x = 200$, $y = 200$.

    ☐ True   ☐ False

Lesson 7
Designing a turtle program using Scratch

1. The 'define' block in Scratch appears when you use which function?

    A   Name a custom block ☐

    B   Create a block ☐

    C   My new block ☐

    D   Make a block ☐

2. Describe the purpose of each block within this custom block program.

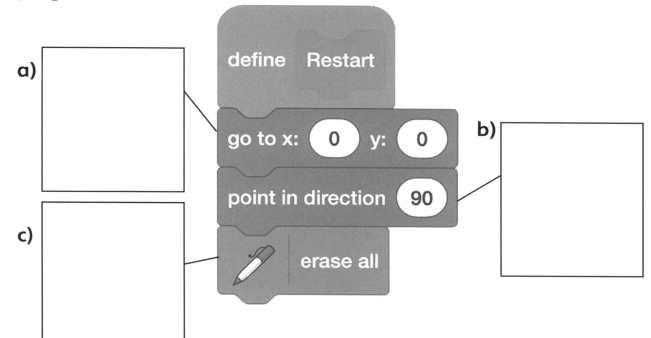

a)

b)

c)

3. Using three custom blocks, which program will create the following pattern? Circle A, B or C.

A

when ▷ clicked

Forward

Forward

Turn right

Forward

Turn left

Turn left

Forward

B

when ▷ clicked

Forward

Turn left

Forward

Turn right

Forward

Turn left

Forward

C

when ▷ clicked

Forward

Turn right

Forward

Turn left

Turn left

Forward

Forward

4. A custom block that would move backwards 30 steps would have which value?

A   30

B   backward 30

C   −30

D   reverse 30

Lessons 8 and 9
Improving and debugging a program using Scratch

1. What is the colour range of the Scratch pen tool?

    A   1–10

    B   black to white

    C   1–100

    D   1–200

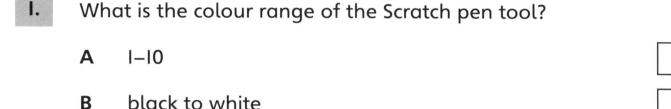

Pen

Draw with your sprites.

2. Match the Scratch blocks to the sections they can be found in.

set pen colour to	Motion
repeat	Pen extension
point in direction 90	Operators
pick random 1 to 10	Control

3. Describe the purpose of the repeat block in Scratch.

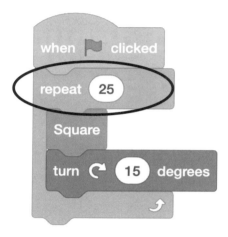

_____

_____

_____

4. Complete the paragraph below about debugging an algorithm. Use the words in the word bank to help you.

(**Tip:** There are more words than you need!)

Word bank
algorithm   block   book   bugs   look   robot   think

The best way to debug an algorithm is

to _____ like a computer.

To debug, read the _____
or code carefully and think how a

_____ would do that
command. Then check again, until you
have checked all of the algorithm and

spotted any _____.

Lesson 10
Creating repeating algorithms using 2D shapes

1. These blocks are part of a larger drawing program.

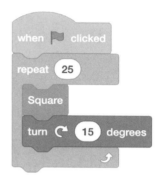

a) What is the name of the defined custom block?

_____

b) What will happen if the program is run?

A 40 squares will be drawn. ☐

B 15 squares will be drawn with a 25 degree turn after each one. ☐

C 25 squares will be drawn in a grid. ☐

D 25 squares will be drawn with a 15 degree turn after each one. ☐

2. What pattern will be created if the following changes are made to the blocks in Question 1? Tick the correct box.

repeat = 4

turn clockwise = 90 degrees

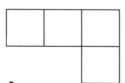   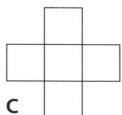   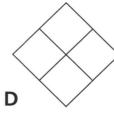

A   **B**   **C**   **D**

☐   ☐   ☐   ☐

3. What can we use repeat blocks for?

   A   to define shapes   ☐

   B   to define colours   ☐

   C   to reduce the number of commands needed   ☐

   D   to debug the program   ☐

4. In Lesson 10, Activity 1 of the Student Book, you made a 2D repeating pattern using Scratch. You created it with squares. What pattern can you make with triangles? Sketch your ideas below. If you have time, perhaps you could try out your idea using Scratch!

Unit 5
End-of-unit assessment

1   An algorithm is a set of _____
    instructions.

    A   basic ☐

    B   precise ☐

    C   vague ☐

    D   complex ☐

(1 mark)

2   Here is an algorithm for opening Scratch on a computer.
    Tick the step that is in the **incorrect** place.

    Open your web browser. ☐

    Type scratch.mit.edu into the address bar
    at the top of the window. ☐

    Turn on the computer. ☐

    Press the 'Enter' key on the keyboard. ☐

(1 mark)

3   Here is an algorithm for a program to draw a rectangle with long sides of 10 cm and short sides of 3 cm.

```
Start

Move forward 3 cm

Turn left 90°

Move forward 10 cm

Turn left 90°

Move forward 6 cm

Turn left 90°

Move forward 10 cm
```

There is an error in the algorithm. What is it?

_____

_____

(I mark)

4   Write the algorithm to draw a square with sides of 4 cm. Use these commands:

```
Move FD (add value in cm)

LT 90

RT 90
```

_____

_____

_____

_____

_____

_____

_____

(3 marks)

5   A student made the custom block below. When the green flag is pressed, the sprite moves but nothing is drawn. Which block has the student forgotten to add?

define   draw a square

repeat   4

move   100   steps

turn ↻   90   degrees

when 🏳 clicked

draw a square

A   [erase all]   ☐

B   [pen down]   ☐

C   [pen up]   ☐

D   [set pen color to ◯]   ☐

(1 mark)

Unit 5 Checkpoints

I can draw 2D shapes by giving correct commands.	☺ ☐ 😐 ☐ ☹ ☐
I can order commands to complete a shape, debugging if necessary.	☺ ☐ 😐 ☐ ☹ ☐
I can make and use custom blocks in a Scratch program.	☺ ☐ 😐 ☐ ☹ ☐
I can plan a program to perform tasks.	☺ ☐ 😐 ☐ ☹ ☐
I can use custom blocks to make geometric patterns.	☺ ☐ 😐 ☐ ☹ ☐

Unit 6

Managing my digital world

In this unit, you will learn about your digital world and how you can control it. You will learn about local, network and cloud storage systems and the good and bad features of each system. You will learn about the use of sensible naming structures, including folders and subfolders, which will help you to save and load files easily. You will also learn about file management, tips for saving files and demonstrate your new learning in a variety of formats.

Lesson 1
The importance of files and folders

1. Files and folders on a computer are often described as like an electronic...

    A   shoe box   ☐

    B   wardrobe   ☐

    C   filing cabinet   ☐

    D   sock drawer   ☐

2. Match the terms to the correct descriptions.

Terms	Descriptions
file	A folder inside another folder.
folder	A collection of folders.
subfolder	Any single document on a computer.
directory	A place to store related files together.

Name
....
  ⌄ Today (1)
....
  📁 New Folder

3. The same terms from Question 2 can also be shown in a diagram. Add labels in the spaces provided.

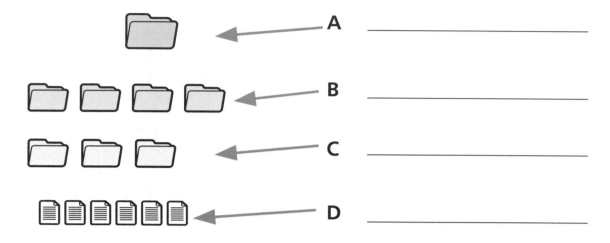

A _____

B _____

C _____

D _____

4. Is the following statement true or false? Tick the correct box.

All documents saved on a computer, from any application, are files.

☐ True   ☐ False

Lesson 2
Managing files and folders (part 1)

1. Tick whether each of the file names in the table below are sensible or not sensible.

Filename	Sensible	Not sensible
22446688		
My art homework		
Document 1		
New file 10		
Forest research		
Space story		

2. What is a naming convention when using files and folders?

_____

_____

📁 Music

📁 Photos

📁 School work

📁 Scratch Programs

📁 Videos

3. Put the steps for creating and renaming a new folder into the correct order by numbering them from I to 5.

☐ Click 'new folder' or right-click and select 'new folder'.

☐ Right-click and select 'rename'.

☐ Open the file explorer application on your device.

☐ Make sure you have chosen the correct place for your folder.

☐ Give your folder a sensible folder name.

4. Is the following statement true or false? Tick the correct box.

> The names of files and folders cannot be changed when using a tablet or smartphone device.

☐ True   ☐ False

📁 superrrrrrrr day todaaaaaayy!!!!

📁 Birthday Party 2021

Lessons 3 and 4
Managing files and folders (part 2)

1. What is another name used to describe the address below?

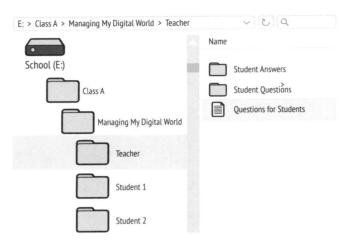

A document route ☐

B file area ☐

C path route ☐

D file path ☐

2. What is the difference between the 'save as' and 'save' command?

_____

_____

_____

_____

3. You would like two copies of a report you have written. Select **two** ways this could be done from the list below.

   A   Open the file and select 'save as' and save to a different folder.   ☐

   B   Right-click on the file, select 'copy' and then select 'paste' in another folder.   ☐

   C   Right-click and select 'rename', choosing a different name.   ☐

   D   Right-click on the file, select 'cut' and then select 'paste' in another folder.   ☐

4. Label the parts of the address shown. Use the words in the word bank to help you.

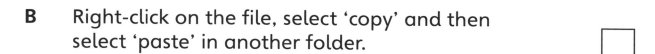

| directory   file   folder   network drive   sub-folder |

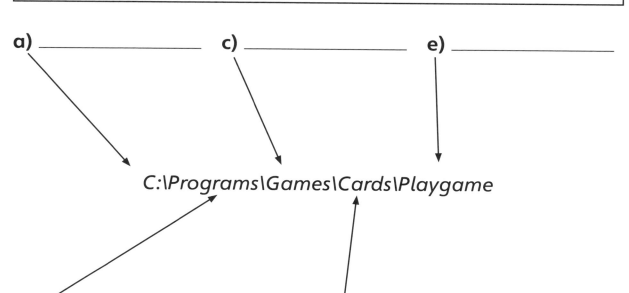

a) _____   c) _____   e) _____

   C:\Programs\Games\Cards\Playgame

b) _____   d) _____

III

Lesson 5
Introduction to online and offline storage

1. List three examples of data we store on a computer.

1 _____

2 _____

3 _____

2. Match the types of storage system to the correct descriptions.

standalone

Files are stored online, in a large internet-connected data centre.

local network

Files are stored online and accessed via the internet.

cloud

Offline storage on your device with no connection to the internet.

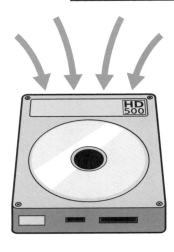

3.   For each of the types of storage below, describe a good thing and a bad thing.

    a) Standalone storage:

       ✓ Good thing: _____

       ✗ Bad thing: _____

    b) Local network storage

       ✓ Good thing: _____

       ✗ Bad thing: _____

    c) Cloud storage

       ✓ Good thing: _____

       ✗ Bad thing: _____

4.   Describe a job where cloud storage could be really useful.

_____

_____

_____

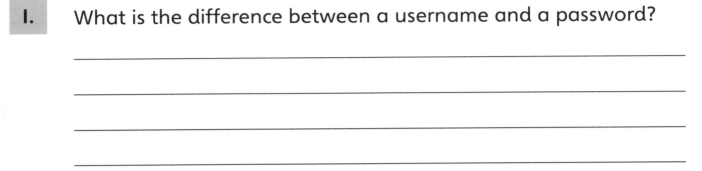

Lesson 6
Keeping your data safe

1. What is the difference between a username and a password?

    _____

    _____

    _____

    _____

LOG-IN

Username: [   ]
Password: [   ]

2. List three examples of online accounts you might have when
    you are much older which will need a good password to access
    them.

    1 _____

    2 _____

    3 _____

3. Give three pieces of advice for creating a strong password.

I _____

_____

2 _____

_____

3 _____

_____

4. List two examples of where we might use a PIN.

I _____

2 _____

5. Many devices use biometrics instead of passwords.

a) Name two examples of biometrics.

I _____

2 _____

b) Describe an example of where they might be used.

_____

Lessons 7 and 8
Creating a digital diagram

1. What is the meaning of the word 'diagram'?

_____

_____

2. List three things that can be added to a diagram to help make it clearer.

1 _____

2 _____

3 _____

3. Name a type of application suitable for creating a diagram.

_____

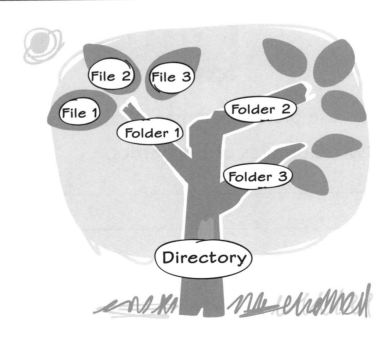

4.   Match the diagram terms to the correct descriptions.

text box	This is used to show that text is linked to a certain part of an image or graphic.
arrow	This is used to place text around the edge of an image.
text wrapping	This is used to move text or images in front of or behind each other.
layering	This is used to move blocks of text around the page easily, create labels and display text in a different way from the rest of the page.

5.   Is the following statement true or false? Tick the correct box.

Diagrams can also be made using pens, pencils and craft materials.

☐ True   ☐ False

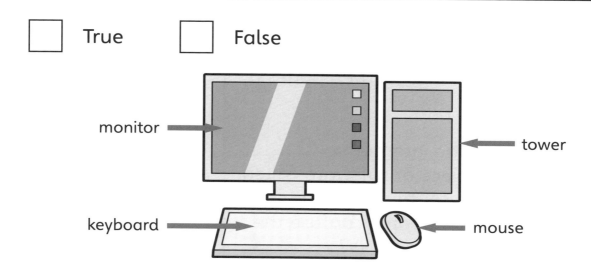

monitor

tower

keyboard

mouse

I. Which of the following is **not** a type of text formatting?

A italic

B bold

C basic

D capitalisation

2. List the text formatting used at each point of the text shown.
(More than one type of formatting may have been used.)

<u>**The internet and the WWW**</u>

The **internet** is the international
network of connected devices
that allows us to communicate
with each other across the world.
The **World Wide Web** describes
all the **web pages** that are
stored on the internet. We call a
group of connected web pages a
website.

<u>Accessing the internet</u>
We use a piece of software called
a web browser to read web
pages. Many people confuse the
internet with the WWW.

a) _____

b) _____

c) _____

d) _____

3. List three topics of new learning from this unit that you could present to your classmates.

1 _____

_____

2 _____

_____

3 _____

_____

4. With a partner or group, think back to other presentations you have given to your class or group. Which application did you use? Would you use the same one for this presentation? Do some applications work better for certain subjects? Create a mind map below to show your thoughts.

Presentations

Unit 6
End-of-unit assessment

1   You are working on a presentation in school and must save your work in the class area. What should you include in your file name?

   A   your pet's name

   B   the day of the week

   C   your best friend's name

   D   your name

(I mark)

2   A folder inside another folder is called a...

   A   subfolder

   B   internal folder

   C   infolder

   D   super folder

(I mark)

3   A student is organising some files on their computer. To the right are the new subfolders.

   📁 Music
   📁 Photos
   📁 School work
   📁 Scratch Programs
   📁 Videos

a)   The student has done some research that they will use in a class presentation. Which folder should they save the file in?

_____

b)　The student has filmed a green screen animation. Which folder should they save the file in?

_____

(2 marks)

4　Which **two** of the following could be described as strong passwords?

A　unicorn ☐

B　password ☐

C　#NOIwIlg3t ☐

D　spR-SpI!! ☐

(2 marks)

5　A teacher working in three different schools saves all their work using online storage. Give one good thing and one bad thing about this method of working.

✓ Good thing: _____

_____

✗ Bad thing: _____

_____

(2 marks)

Unit 6 Checkpoints

I can save work regularly and keep information secure.	🙂	☐
	😐	☐
	☹️	☐
I can use sensible file names.	🙂	☐
	😐	☐
	☹️	☐
I can organise files into directories, folders and subfolders.	🙂	☐
	😐	☐
	☹️	☐
I understand how to use usernames and passwords to secure data.	🙂	☐
	😐	☐
	☹️	☐
I can choose and use different software applications.	🙂	☐
	😐	☐
	☹️	☐